Level Four
(D / Grade 2½)

John W. Schaum presents the

I0798706

BEST of BACH

For Piano Solo

Foreword

The primary object of this album is to serve as an *introduction* to the music of Bach. Therefore, emphasis is placed on *melodic* works, rather than on polyphony, because melody is more easily comprehended by the student at this grade level. The polyphonic aspect of Bach is better suited for a more advanced level of achievement.

The choice of music in the collection is determined by its effectiveness for *teaching* purposes — based on thirty five years' experience with thousands of piano students at the Schaum Music School in Wisconsin.

Additional books in this series are:

Best of BEETHOVEN
Best of BRAHMS
Best of CHOPIN
Best of MOZART
Best of RACHMANINOFF
Best of SCHUBERT
Best of TCHAIKOWSKY

SCHAUM PUBLICATIONS, INC.
10235 N. Port Washington Rd. • Mequon, WI 53092
www.schaumpiano.net

07-11
AJ-26

Biographical Sketch

Although Bach lived only three centuries ago he is one of the earliest of the great musicians; for music is the youngest of all the arts. When the great poets, sculptors and painters of ancient times lived and worked there was nothing in all the world corresponding to what we know as music. The art of music is hardly more than three centuries old.

Johann Sebastian Bach was born in Eisenach, Germany, March 21, 1685. Bach's father was a violinist, and very naturally taught him first to play on his own instrument. In Johann's tenth year both parents died and he went to live with his elder brother who was a church organist in another city.

Under his brother's direction he started the study of the clavier (clavier is the German name for any stringed instrument played by means of a keyboard). He quickly mastered all of his lessons demonstrating his great talent and genius.

When Bach was fifteen years old he was sent to school in Lüneburg, where his outstanding vocal ability enabled him to earn his tuition by singing in the church choir. At the age of twenty three, he was appointed court organist at Weimar, where he became famed as the greatest player of his time; and there he composed much of his organ music.

But the clavichord was Bach's favorite instrument. It was one of the old-fashioned keyboard instruments that was used before the piano was invented. Its sweet delicate tone was produced by striking the keys which in turn pressed little wedges against the strings.

Bach developed a special way of tuning the clavichord. He called it "Well-Tempered" meaning 'evenly-tuned.' It was for this instrument that Bach wrote his monumental series of compositions entitled, "The Well-Tempered Clavichord." All keyboard instruments are now tuned according to Bach's system. His method of tuning and his style of composing has made possible the present high development of the art of music.

Index

My Heart Ever Faithful

J. S. BACH
Arr. by John W. Schaum

Moderato

Jesu, Joy of Man's Desiring

J. S. BACH
Arr. by John W. Schaum

mf cantabile
p
mf cantabile
p

Siciliano

Siciliano (pronounced see-sil-YAH-no) is a graceful rustic dance which originated in Sicily.

J. S. BACH
Arr. by John W. Schaum

mf a tempo
p
rit.

Bourrée

Bourreé (pronounced boo-RAY) is a lively old French dance tune.

J. S. BACH
Arr. by John W. Schaum

Allegro

cresc.

Gavotte

Gavotte (pronounced gah-VAHT) is a dance of French peasant origin which was introduced at court in the 16th century.

J. S. BACH
Arr. by John W. Schaum

March in D Major

J. S. BACH
Arr. by John W. Schaum

Sheep May Safely Graze

J. S. BACH
Arr. by John W. Schaum

rit.

Prelude No. 1 (Ave Maria)

This "Prelude," the first of Bach's monumental work "The Well Tempered Clavichord," has been ingeniously utilized by Gounod as an accompaniment to his popular "Ave Maria." It is thus probably better known to music lovers than any other of Bach's compositions.

In the following piano arrangement, the student may play the "Prelude" as a solo or as a duet in combination with the "Ave Maria."

J. S. BACH
Arr. by John W. Schaum

cresc.
f
mf
mf
p

cresc. molto
f
mf
cresc.
rit.
rit.

Musette

Musette (pronounced myou-ZET) means literally a bagpipe. It refers to music appropriate to a bagpipe.

J. S. BACH
Arr. by John W. Schaum

Air for G String

J. S. BACH
Arr. by John W. Schaum

Andante cantabile

p
cresc.
p
cresc.
mf
p
cresc.
f
p
rit.
pp

Minuet in G Major

Edward MacDowell in his teaching at Columbia University made a medley of these two minuets on pages 20 and 21. Try it, by playing page 20, page 21 and then back to page 20 without any rhythmic pause between.

J. S. BACH
Arr. by John W. Schaum

Minuet in G Minor

J.S. BACH
Arr. by John W. Schaum

Allegretto

Prelude in C Minor

J. S. BACH
Arr. by John W. Schaum

cresc.
f
dim.
p
cresc.
f
rit.
f

THEMES by the MASTERS ... Every Student Should Know

All Titles — LEVEL FOUR

- Music Selected for its EFFECTIVENESS in TEACHING
- Each Book Includes BIOGRAPHICAL DATA and COMPOSER PORTRAIT
- Collections Include Themes from SYMPHONIES, CHAMBER MUSIC, VOCAL LITERATURE, OPERA and PIANO

BEST OF BACH

INCLUDES: Air for G String — Bouree
Gavotte — Jesu, Joy of Man's Desiring
March in D Major — Minuet in G Major
Minuet in G Minor — Musette
My Heart Ever Faithful — Siciliano

BEST OF BEETHOVEN

INCLUDES: Andante from 5th Symphony
Bagatelle — Ecossaise — Fur Elise
Heavens Declare His Glory
Minuet from Sonata Op.49, No.2
Minuet in G — Moonlight Sonata

BEST OF MOZART

INCLUDES: Air in C (Marriage of Figaro)
Allegro in B-flat, K3 — Lullaby
Hand in Hand (Don Giovanni)
Minuet (Symphony in E-flat)
Overture (Marriage of Figaro)

Excerpt from "BEST OF BEETHOVEN"

BEST OF SCHUBERT

CONTENTS:
Cradle Song
Hark, Hark, the Lark
Impromptu, Op.142, No.2
Love Theme (from "Unfinished Symphony")
March Militaire
Minuet from Sonata, Op.78
Moment Musical, Op.94, No.3
Rosamunde Ballet Music, Op.26
Serenade
Sweet Repose (Du bist die Ruh')
Theme from Octet, Op.166
Trout
Valses Nobles, Op.77
Waltz in C

BEST OF TCHAIKOWSKY

CONTENTS:
Chanson Triste
Eugene Onegin Waltz
Italian Caprice
March Slav
None But the Lonely Heart
Piano Concerto Theme
Romance
Romeo and Juliet Love Theme
Serenade for Strings
Sleeping Beauty Waltz
Song Without Words
Swan Lake Finale
Sweet Dreams
Waltz from Swan Lake